PARACOl

Beginners Guide to Paracord Techniques and Projects with Pictorial Project Guide on Bucklers, Bracelets, Keychains, Monkey Fist, Belts, Lanyards, and other Ropecrafting Projects

Todd Brian

Copyright@2022

Table of Contents

CHAPTER ONE

Introduction

DIY Ladder Made of Cord and Wooden Rungs

In this book, I'll show you how to make various projects, starting with this first one on how to make a rope ladder out of standard paracord and wooden rungs. Rope ladders can be used for almost anything, from tree houses to boats to haylofts. They can also be used as fire escapes in the event of a fire. This is also one of my entries for the paracord contest, so please read carefully all the projects in this book and try to make them yourself following my instructions step by step!

Step 1: Create a Bill of Materials

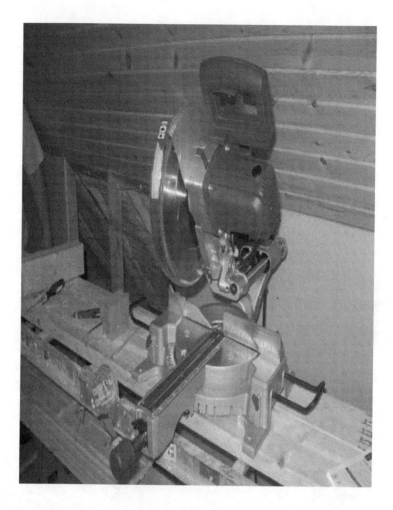

Here's what you'll need:

Corduroy (see step 2 for exact amount)

Wooden dowels (see step 2 for exact amount)

Where to buy your materials:

I purchased my paracord from a local military surplus store for 9 cents per foot. You can also get 300' of it for $13, which is a much better deal.

Wood - Available at your local hardware store, Home Depot, Lowe's, or equivalent.

You'll need dowels because the knot I'm using requires a circular surface. I used a number one "dowel, but make sure it can support your entire body.

Tools:

Chopsaw/TableSaw

Hammer/Nail

Step 2: Gathering the Materials

At this step, you must decide how tall you want your rope ladder to be. There is no formula for determining how much rope you require. Take the desired height, multiply it by two, and add 10-20'. Because of the knots in the paracord, you'll need more. You'll need one rung every 8-12 inches. In terms of width, it actually depends on the application. I made my rungs 8 "I made them broad in order to make them stronger.

Step 3: Trim the Rungs

After that, you'll need to cut the rungs off the dowel. I was meant to get 6, but I had some problems with the saw and only got 5. This step is relatively self-explanatory; simply make a mark on the dowel where you want to cut and cut. ALWAYS WEAR SAFETY GLASSES!

Step 4: Making the Paracord

Now, take your paracord and shape it into a very narrow U-shape, as seen below.

Mark the middle or bottom of the U with masking tape.

Step 5: Learning to Tie a Knot

The knot we'll be using is known as the constrictor knot, and we've included some illustrations to help you master it. Before you use it on the ladder, practice a few times. You need it to be tight and cost-effective.

This knot is quite strong when tightened. You can also use the double constrictor, but keep in mind that it will require more rope.

Step 6: Tying the Rungs

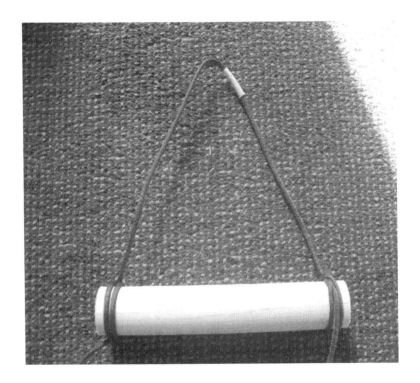

Tie the paracord around the dowel using the constrictor knot. Try to keep the spacing on either side of the dowel roughly the same; you can fine-tune later. This is where the tape comes in handy.

Make the two sides leading to the first rung the same length. This will assist you in keeping your ladder balanced. When you're finished, make sure all of the knots are tightened and properly aligned so they don't slide.

When you step on it for the first time, they may slide, but simply fine-tune the knots to eliminate the unbalance.

Step 7: Continue Down the Ladder

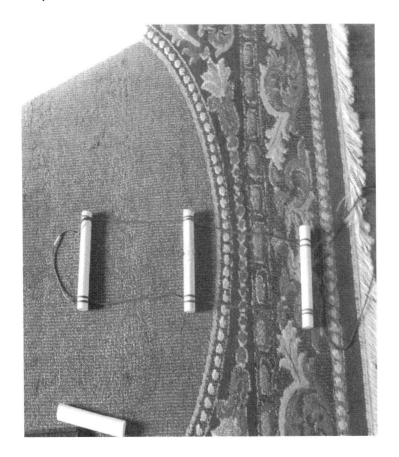

Simply repeat this step until you are finished. Keep spacing in mind, and try to make it all equal.

Step 8: Assembling the Ladder

There are numerous ways to mount the ladder. Some people may choose to mount it on the inside of their windows as a fire escape. I chose to test it for the time being by punting in a 3 "In my barn, I used a nail to attach to a solid beam.

Keep in mind that this is NOT the best or safest way to mount it, but it worked well enough for testing. If you do this, try to tilt the nail so that it holds better. Caution: When I tested my ladder, I used an adjacent ladder to support myself in case the paracord ladder broke. Don't just assume it's strong enough!

Step 9: You're Done!

This ladder can be used for a variety of purposes, including emergency escape, building a treehouse, or simply having a rope ladder!

-Braid the paracord to make it stronger.

-Use higher-quality wood for the rungs.

-At the top, attach a wooden mounting bracket.

-Find a way to secure the knots so they don't slide around as much.

Thank you for reading my guide; please patronize and rate!

CHAPTER TWO

DIY Christmas Tree Ball Ornament Using Paracord

Frequently, paracord is referred to as a military cord or survival equipment. Today, this strong nylon rope is available in an infinite variety of colors and designs, making it ideal for both ornamental and functional use.

One such application is as a Christmas tree ornament ball. Whether you're into paracord making or simply want an ornament that is genuinely indestructible, these will look fantastic on any Christmas tree. Customize the colors to match your design plan precisely!

If you're new to paracord crafting, this project may take up to two hours. This could easily be completed in 30 minutes by an expert.

Step 1: Materials

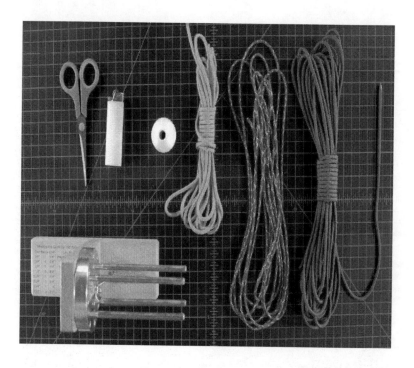

To create this decoration, you will need the following materials:

• Paracord hues for the holidays (Tinsel paracord is real)

• 1.5-inch ping-pong ball "bead made of wood

• Jig with monkey fists

- paracord fidget spinner

- Lighter

- Scissors

Paracord Planet offers a wide variety of paracord colors.

Ping pong balls are an excellent choice for the ornament's center. The ornament is lighter, the easier it is to put on your tree. When I was a child, I recall attempting to get metal decorations to stay on our scrawny Christmas tree. It was a constant effort to keep them from falling to the floor!

Monkeying Around in Step 2

Monkey Fist Guide For 550 Paracord

Core	Passes	Cord	Core	Passes	Cord
5/8"	3	1' 8"	Ping Pong	8	10' 2"
3/4"	4	2' 6"	15/8"	9	11' 2"
7/8"	5	3' 4"	Golf Ball	9	11' 10"
1"	5	4' 4"	13/4"	9	12' 10"
11/8"	6	5' 4"	17/8"	10	14' 8"
11/4"	7	6' 8"	2"	11	16' 10"
13/8"	7	8'	21/8"	11	19'
11/2"	8	9' 6"	21/4"	11	21' 4"

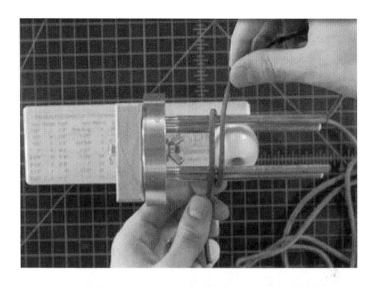

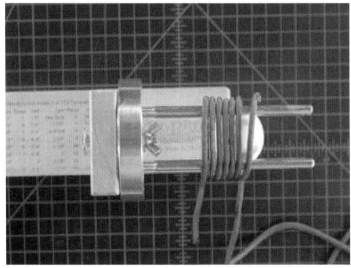

A monkey fist jig simplifies this project significantly. If you don't have a jig, you can still make it, but it will be more difficult. Take a look at this monkey fist keychain guide for video instructions on how to build a monkey fist without a jig.

Begin by wrapping the paracord around the monkey fist jig's top two posts. Continue wrapping it around each of the four posts until you reach a total of eight wraps. Come to a halt at the exact point where you began.

It is worth noting that if you do not use a 1.5 in "You will have a different number of passes for the core. The chart illustrates the number of passes required for 550 paracord on various core sizes.

The Third Step: A New Direction

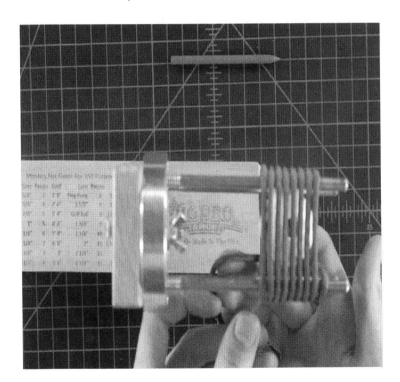

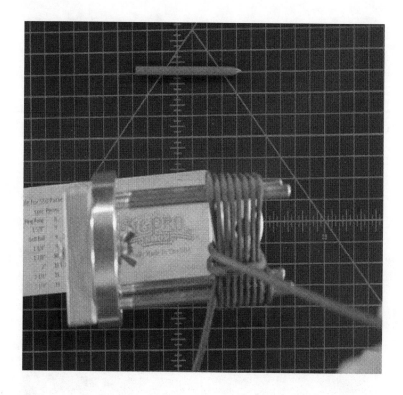

The second vertical wrap begins now. Prior to starting, insert your core (the bead or the ping-pong ball). Wrap the cable downward around the initial post. Bring the cord up between the posts and around the bottom toward the left. This wrap occurs left to right in the images. Complete eight wraps in this way, stopping at the opposite top post from where you began.

Step 4: Continue indefinitely

We still have one additional direction to wrap. This one is a little unique in comparison to the other two. Rather than covering over everything, this wrap goes underneath and above.

If you have a fid, attach it to the paracord's working end. Insert the paracord beneath the first direction wraps in the corner where you completed the second direction, pointing your fid toward the base of the jig posts. Return on the opposite side, this time beneath the first direction's wraps. Continue downward until you have a total of eight wraps in this last direction.

Step 5: The *Not-So-Enjoyable* Part

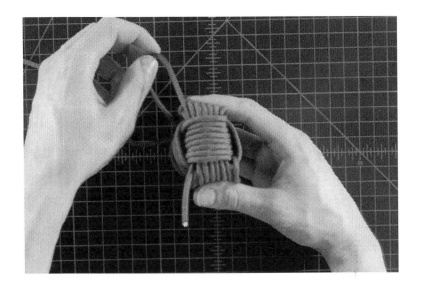

It is now time to remove your monkey fist from the jig. If constructed properly, it will retain its shape.

You're finished with the wrapping, but not with the ornament. This section may become a little messy. Now is the time to clench the monkey fist. This can only be accomplished by threading the cord through one strand at a time. You may need to repeat this technique several times to ensure that the knot is entirely secure.

Begin with the paracord's short end.
Continue pulling until the cord protrudes 2
"'. Continue to feed the cord through the
knot one wrap at a time. This process is
usual to take some time, so be patient.

Step 6: Eggnog Refreshment

You've worked hard to get here, so reward
yourself! Take a seat, sip some egg nog,
sing a few carols, and warm your toes by
the fire. Then, when you're ready, return
your attention to your paracord.

Step 7: A Simple Trim

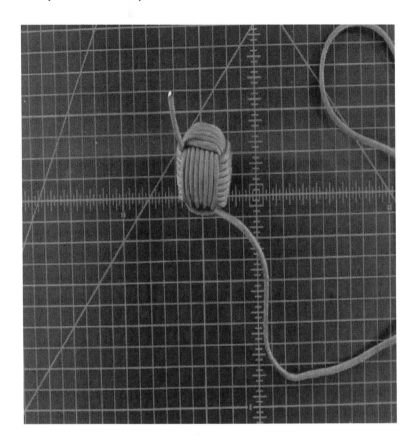

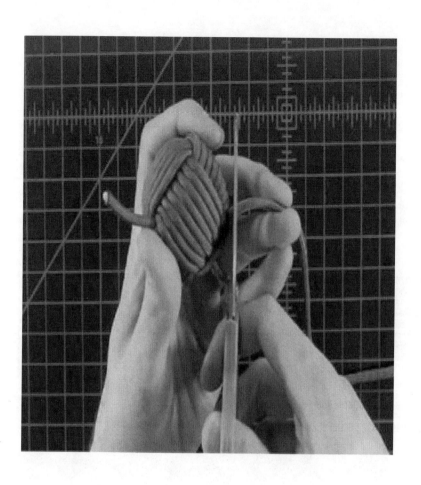

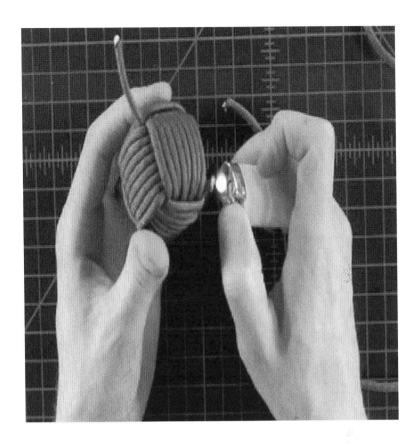

You can now trim the ends. If this is your first time working with paracord, there is a specific technique for completing the ends of your cord.

• To begin, trim the excess rope to about 1/4 inch "keep your monkey fist away from your face.

• Melt the end by holding it near a lighter's flame. Take cautious not to hold it in for an extended period of time. If the paracord's end becomes black, shorten the amount of time it is held in the flame the next time.

• Before the paracord cools, flatten it against your monkey fist with the side of your lighter or scissors.

You'll repeat this procedure following step 9.

Step 8: Concluding (Part 1)

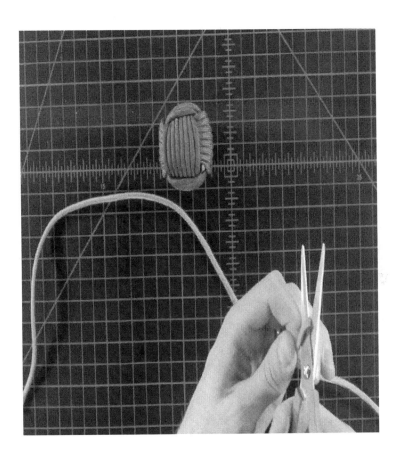

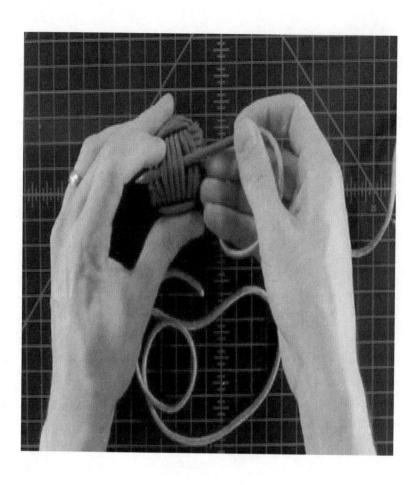

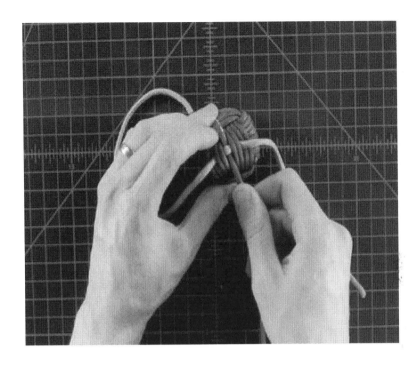

If you wish to just finish the ornament with a bead, you can! I enjoy using a sinnet knot to mimic the metal top of a glass ball ornament.

Cut two 1.5 ft. (45 cm) lengths of metallic paracord. I used the color "goldenrod" from Paracord Planet in these images.

The first cord should be threaded onto your fid. You may need to use your fingers to melt the ends of your rope and trim them to a point. However, exercise caution since it is quite easy to burn your fingers on molten nylon! Pinch your fist beneath the four central cords on either side of your monkey fist.

Transfer your fist to the other severed cord. Pinch this one between the same side's middle two cords. Substitute it for your first metallic cord. Four even strands should now grow from the top of your monkey fist.

Two cords opposite one another should be looped around the top of the decoration to the opposite side. To maintain instructional continuity, position your right-to-left cord as far away from you as possible, as seen in the illustration.

Then, using the other pair of opposite cords, repeat the procedure—with one exception. Bring the bottom cord over the first but not the second cord. Ascertain that it is positioned to the right of the top cord. Then, with the top cord, repeat the procedure: over the first, under the second.

At this point, all four cords should be entangled. You may remember this pattern from when you were a child and made plastic lace keychains at summer camp. Tighten this down little, but only slightly.

Step 9: Concluding (Part 2)

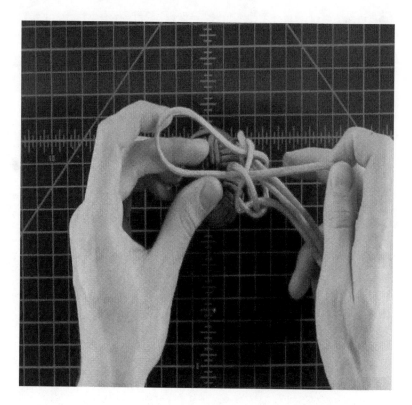

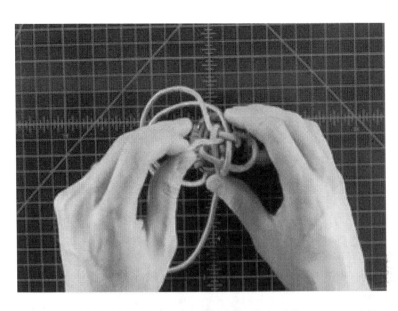

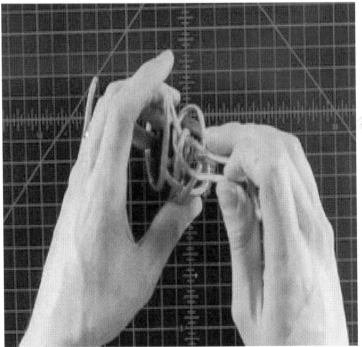

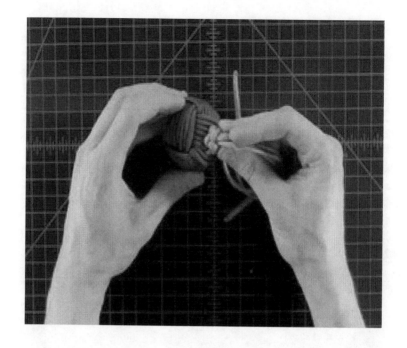

Each rope must now ascend through the center. If you're following along with the illustrations, grab any cord and work your way counter-clockwise beyond one base strand before bringing the cord up through the center of the knot. Carry do this procedure with all four cords.

Now you may tighten the knot by evenly pulling all threads. Once the knot is mostly secure, you can tighten it further by pulling the ropes one by one.

Two cords are required to create the hanging loop in the next phase, so choose two cords and cut them, following the methods in step 7 to melt and finish them.

Step 10: Suspend Everything

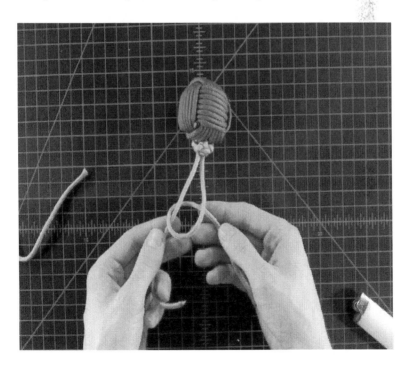

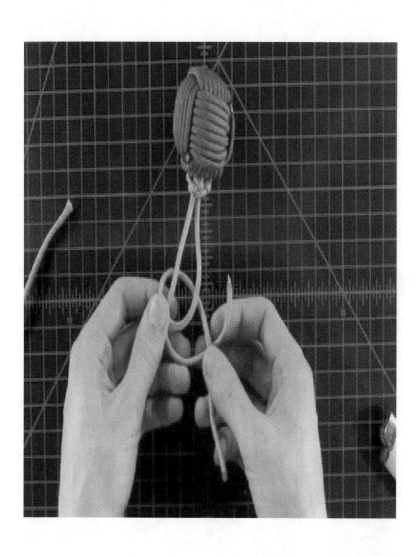

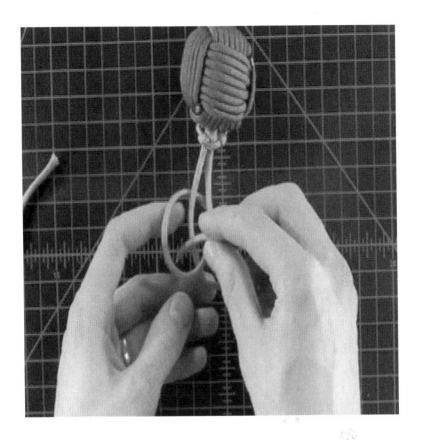

To hang the ornament from your tree, a hanging loop will need to be created.

I prefer a double snake knot to a double overhand knot because it appears more even.

To tie a snake knot, follow these steps:

• Wrap the right-side chord around the left-side cord, such that the tail end is wrapped around the rear.

• Then, bring the left cord behind the right and across the front to the leftmost loop.

• Tighten the knot at a distance of around 2-3" from the ornament.

Create two of these knots and tighten the second one against the first. As previously, cut and melt your ends.

11th Step: Adorn the Tree

That is all. You're finished! Hang your ornament and consume the remainder of your carton of egg nog...

CHAPTER THREE

DIY Wrap a paracord strap

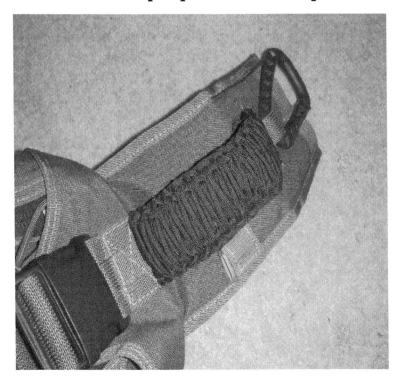

Using various lengths of paracord, the Paracord Strap Wrap is an easy method to tidy up stray ends on your gear. Using paracord in place of common items such as cable ties offers obvious advantages for any paracord enthusiast.

Depending on the length of the strap and the thickness desired, you can use anywhere from 2 or 3 meters to 15 meters.

Step 1:

Now, I've discovered that the majority of the webbing straps on my outdoor gear have a small enough gap at the end to put a single piece of paracord through. The simplest method is to use a cable tie.

Step 2:

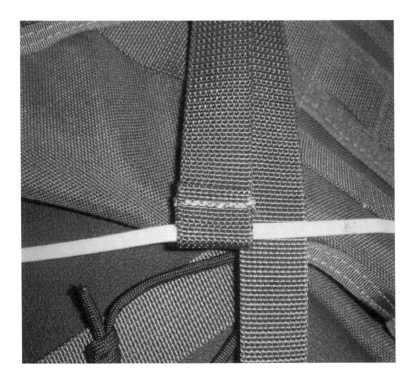

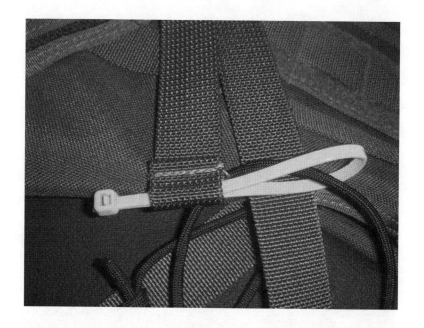

Thread the end without the clip through the end of the strap and back on itself to create a loop. Then, thread paracord through the cable tie loop and pull the tie through completely (pulling the paracord through with it). Then pull the cord through until it reaches around halfway.

Step 3:

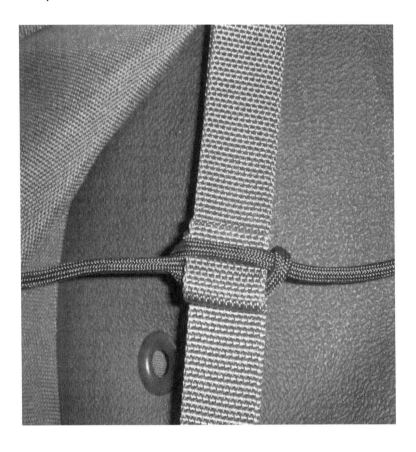

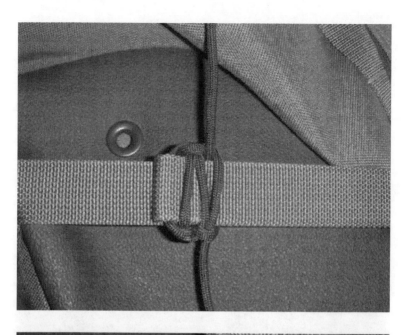

This is based on a stitch I saw in an old knot book; it's called the Cobra stitch, though I've seen it referred to by other names. This is how survival straps are constructed; one end is threaded in front of a core, the other behind it, and then each end is threaded through the loop generated. The strap serves as the central component in this case.

Continue tying loops in until you have several in a row.

Step 4:

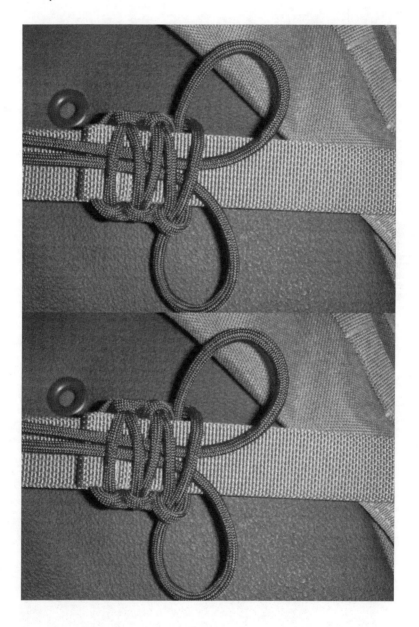

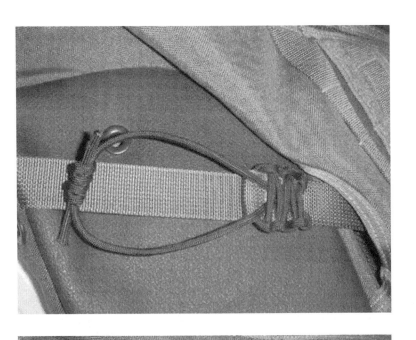

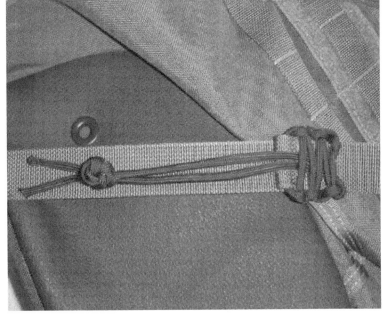

When you're satisfied with the number of loops you've tied off, thread both ends back down the middle and underneath the loops you've tied. A pair of pliers may be necessary depending on the tightness of the loops. Additionally, you may beef it up a bit by going back and making a second or third layer. It can be finished in any way you wish, I tried it with a fisherman's not and a figure of eight, but the final appearance is entirely up to you.

Step 5:

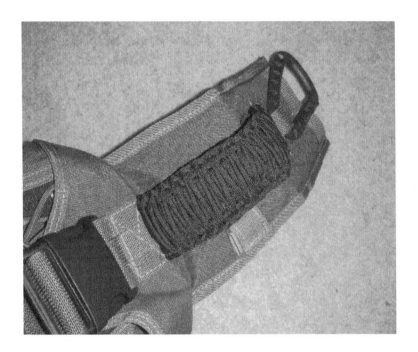

Once you're satisfied with the end knot, clip the ends and use a lighter to wax them. I created two of these on the gearslinger's cross straps and then layered them with a double one on the grab handle.

CHAPTER FOUR

IPhone Case Constructed with Paracord

Step 1: Begin Creating the Outline

You'll need to determine the length of paracord you'll need for the project based on the size of your iPhone. Then begin constructing the side.

Wrapping It in Step 2

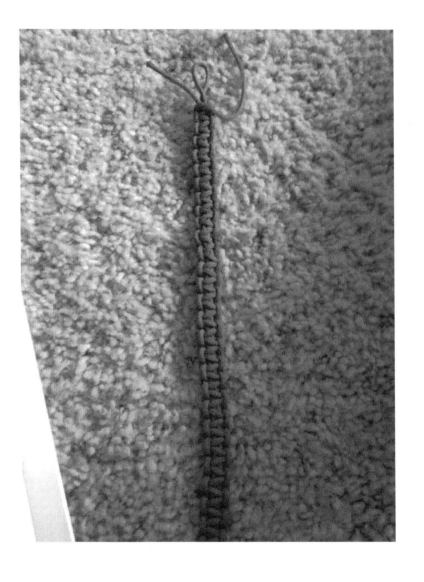

After that, wrap the cords around and tie them.

Step 3: Back Threading

Thread the back up and down and then side to side.

Step 4: Front Ties

Once the back is complete, flip it over and tie the front.

CHAPTER FIVE

Spool Knit Paracord Lanyard - Do It Yourself

Now that that is out of the way, let us begin by following along with me as I explain.

The First Step: What You'll Need

Needed materials/tools for this project:

* +-35ft of paracord in a single color (I started with 50ft but I had about 15ft left over because I felt that 50ft made the lanyard too long)

* a cigarette lighter (to melt the ends of the paracord so it wont unravel [caution when melting ends the molten paracord is very hot and can stick to skin causing 2nd degree burns so be careful])

* shears

* a little screw driver (or other pointed
instrument) for lifting cable.

* a key chain

* a circular device with three pegs; I used
this screw-in for something I discovered
while rummaging around the garage, but
you could also use three little nails softly
hammered into a napkin holder.

The Second Step: Getting Started

To begin, insert a small piece of paracord
through the spool (an inch or two is
sufficient), then wrap the cord twice around
each peg.

Once it is complete, draw the lower cable that is wrapped around the peg over the upper cord, repositioning the lower chord in the spool's middle you should start on the first peg you wrapped so you have the more slack.

The cord is now looped around again and the technique is repeated until the required length is reached.

Step 3: Complete the Knit

To complete the knit, take the last strand you were working on out, then wrap the free strand around the next occupied peg, loop the lower cord over the upper cord, and pull the top strand out similarly to the previous peg. Once the final peg is completed, remove the spool and pull taut... you are now finished with the knit and ready to go on to the weave.

Attaching the Knit to the Key Ring in Step 4

Now you'll need to melt the two ends of the knit together (molten paracord is extremely hot and will burn!), then loop them onto the key ring, making sure to keep the two ends of the knit together or the looping will fail. To hold the two together, wrap the other colored paracord around them at their midpoint.

5th Step: Weave

I'll direct you to step five of stormdrane's paracord bracelet guide for this stage.

Sixth step:

After you've completed that, you're ready
to add your keys and other items. I hope
you enjoyed my guide and please leave me
any helpful ideas or suggestions to help
make my next GUIDE more useful.

CHAPTER SIX

DIY Simple Paracord Bracelet - Cobra Advanced

That bracelet is so simple to manufacture yet is undeniably eye-catching!

You can also use regular Paracord in place of the thin cord!

Difficulty: simple

Material consumption: less

Step 1: Material

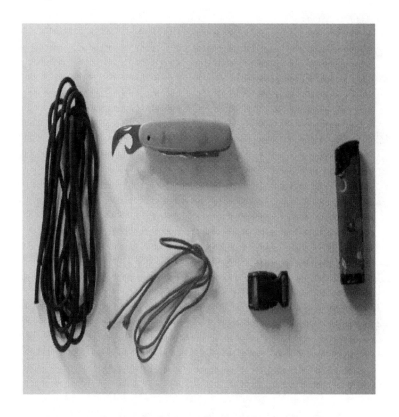

I use approximately 8 feet of black
Paracord to make a standard cobra-
bracelet. Perhaps you should use more, as
my wrist is quite thin.

The thin paracord is type I, which is approximately 2mm in diameter. I ended up using little more than 2 feet of it.

The buckle is 5/8" in diameter, but smaller sizes are available upon request.

Finally, you're going to employ something akin to a hook.

Step 2: Cobra-Knot

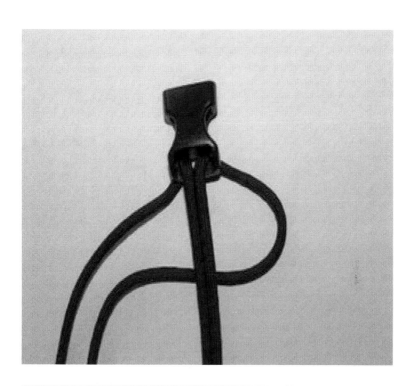

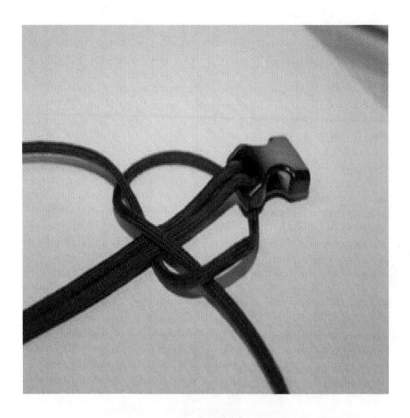

The cobra-knot is the fundamental knot for this bracelet. This is accomplished by placing the right cord beneath the inner cords (the middle ones) on the left. The left cable is then passed beneath (!) the first, over the inner cords, and through the loop on the right side.

ATTENTION! This is the first knot you'll encounter. Therefore, when you tighten it, you have complete control over the bracelet's length! It is possible that something has changed.

Step 3: The Fine Cord

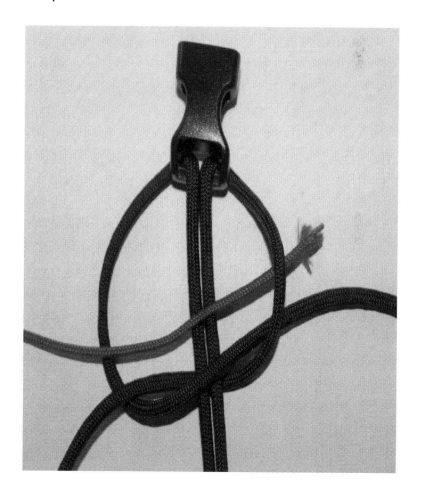

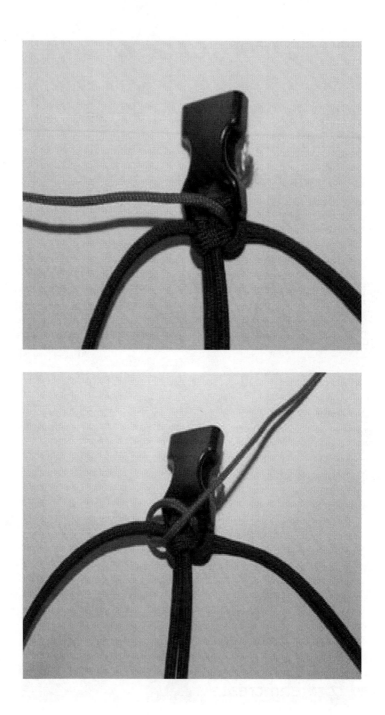

It's now time to attach the thin Paracord. Simply thread one end through the appropriate loop.

When removing the cobra knot from the thigh, take care not to yank it out again!

To tie the second knot, create a loop around the black cord as shown in illustration 3. Following that, disregard the red cord and create a cobra-knot with the black cords (this time you take the left cord first and put it under the inner cords).

Step 4: Continue and Continue...

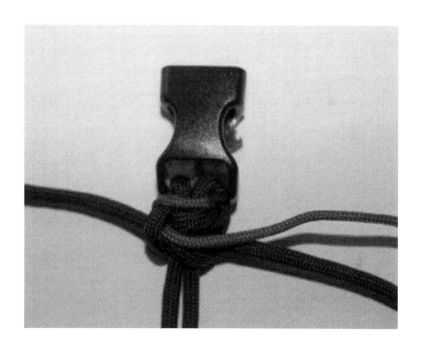

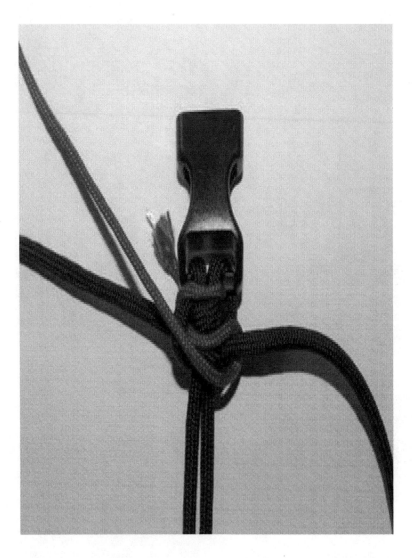

Simply repeat the knot until it is complete.

Step 5: The Final Step

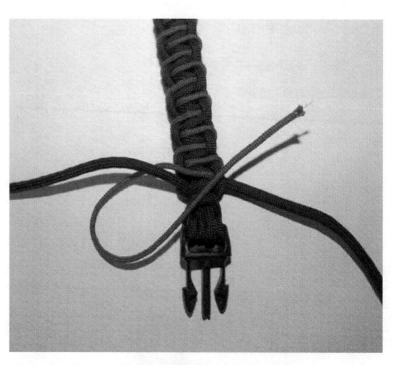

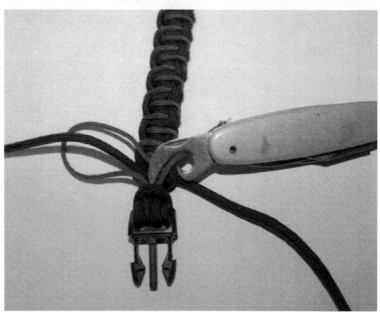

Now that you're almost completed, take your hook and thread it through the inner cords. Finish with a cobra-knot, then cut and burn the cords.

Step 6: DONE!

Congrats!

You can also use a standard cord! It appears to be incredible.

CHAPTER SEVEN

DIY Paracord Pouch for Leatherman PS4 or Gerber Dime Multi-Tools

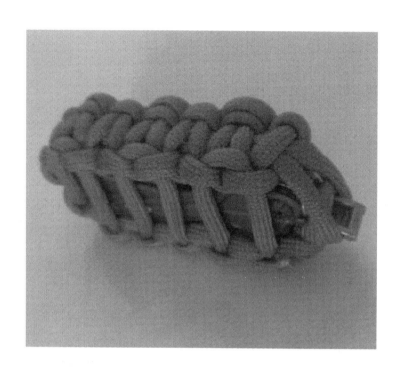

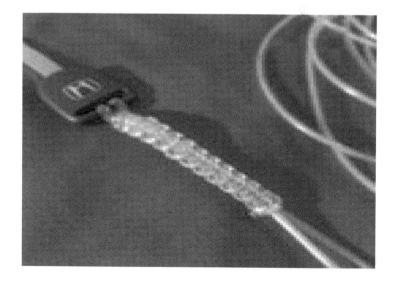

A man must safeguard his tool.

Make a Cobra Weave Bat in Step 1

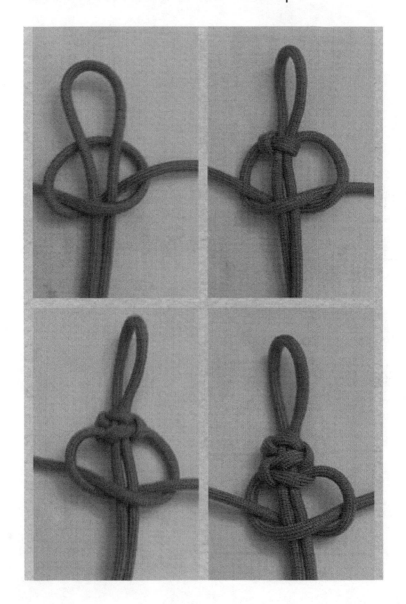

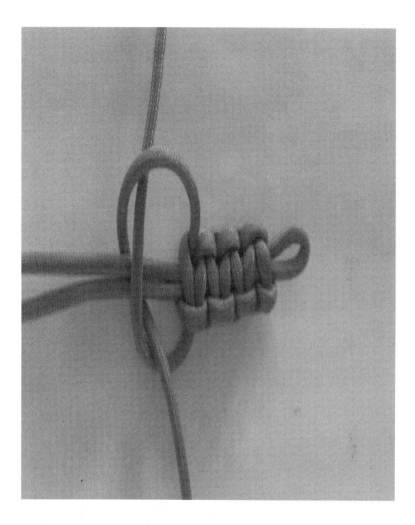

Making a cobra weave bar is similar to making a paracord bracelet.

Step two:

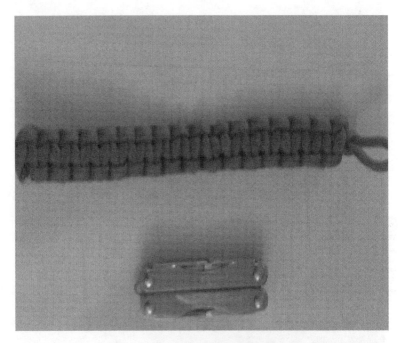

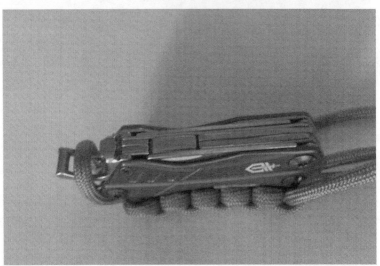

The cobra weave bar will serve as the pouch's primary framework.

3rd Step: Length

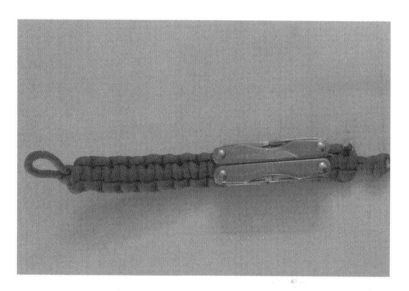

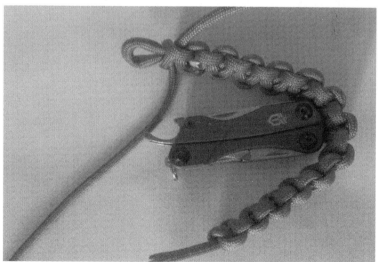

Ascertain that the cobra weave bar is long enough to wrap around the tool's perimeter, leaving one side free for the pouch's mouth.

Step 4: Adjacent Walls

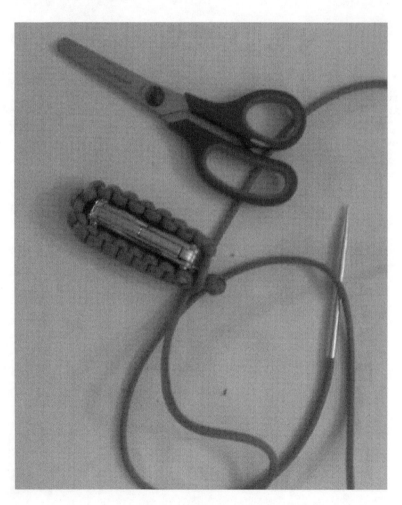

Weave the side of the pouch in and out
with a paracord lacing needle, as shown in
the picture.

Step 5: Adjacent Walls

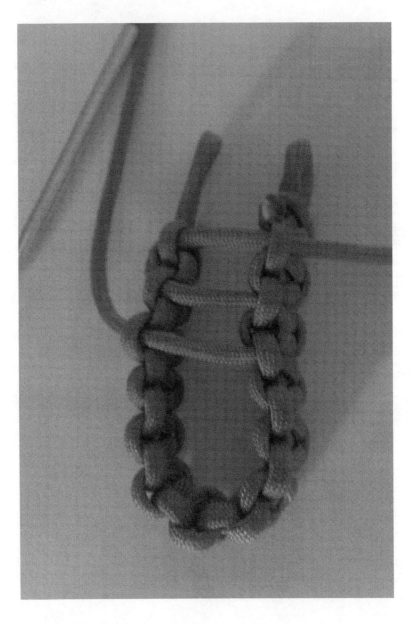

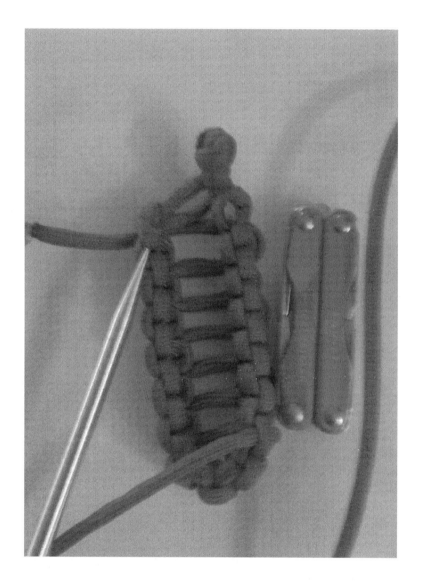

Continue weaving from the pouch's mouth to the bottom, then cross to the opposite side and weave from bottom to top.

Adjustment step 6

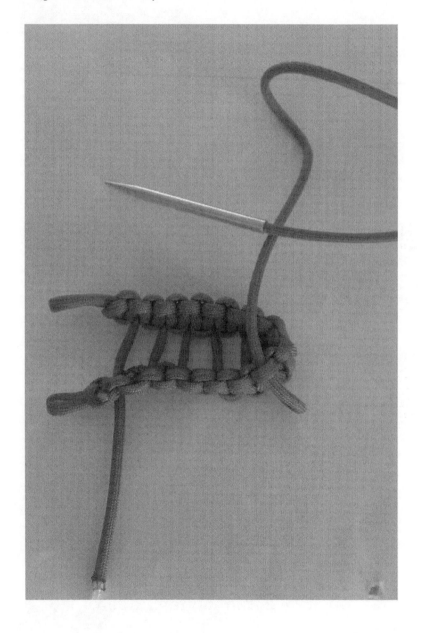

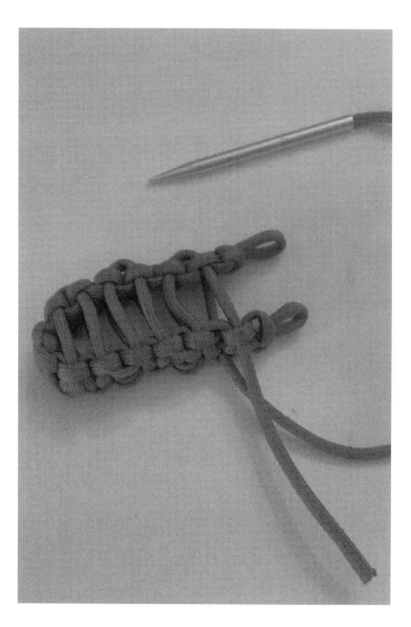

Continue.

Fitting in step 7

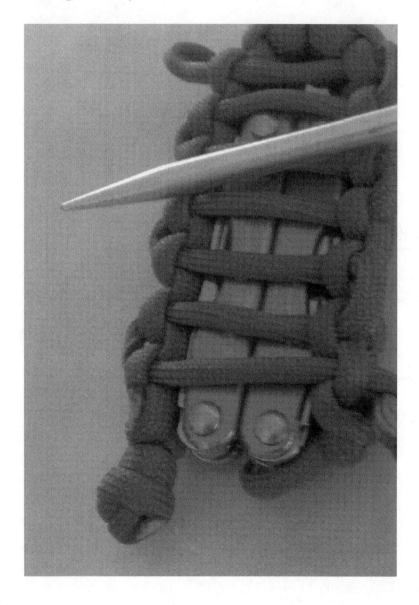

Place the tool inside the bag and adjust the side weaving as necessary to ensure a snug fit.

Step 8: Completion

Tie the ends of the side weaving together, remove any extra, and melt the ends with a lighter.

Voila

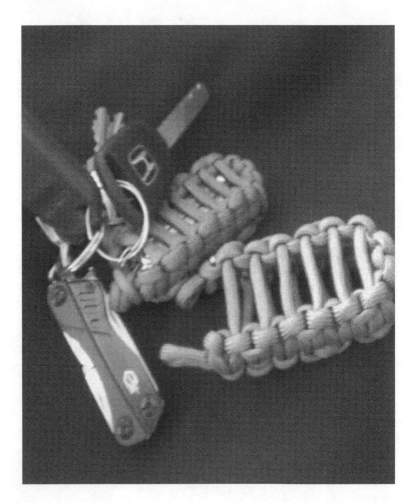

Surprisingly, it is compatible with the Gerber Dime Multi tool as well.

Did you create this project with me following my instructions?
CONGRATULATION

CHAPTER EIGHT

DIY Paracord Monkey Fist

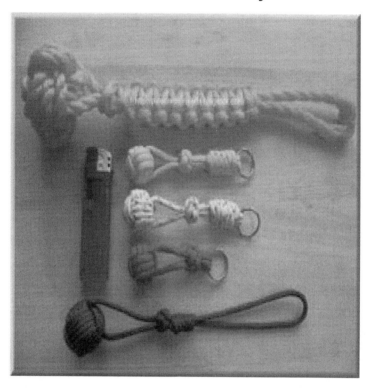

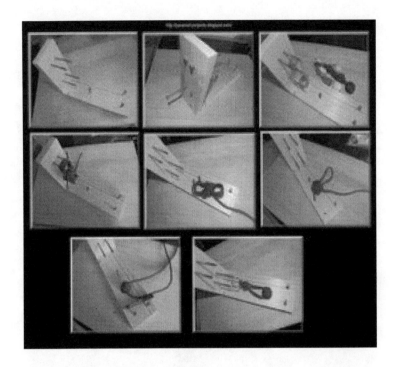

For a long time, people used the Monkey Fist knot as a weight at the end of a rope or to make it look pretty. It has been used since the 1800s.

It was also used as a weapon by sailors and gangs.

A marble is used to make the Monkey Fist in this guide.

Some of your first attempts could go wrong. This knot takes a lot of patience, so take your time, especially when you're tightening the knot at the very end. Do it slowly, and you'll get a cool monkey fist.

Step 1: You can choose Monkey Fist Guide.

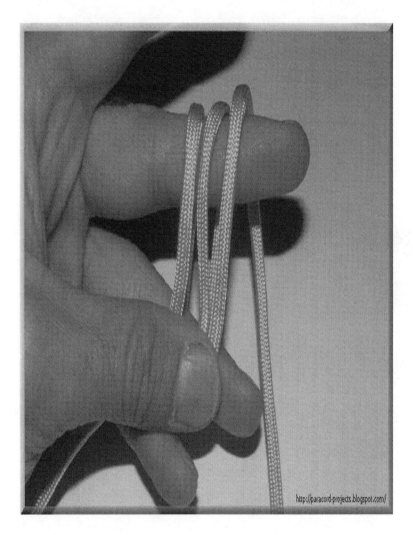

There are many things that could be used inside the knot, but I used a marble.

Step two:

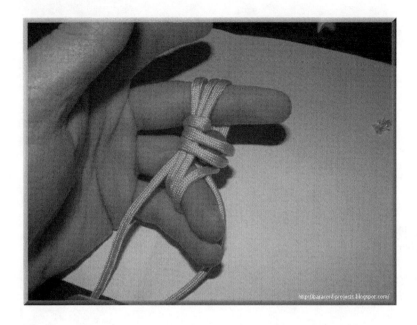

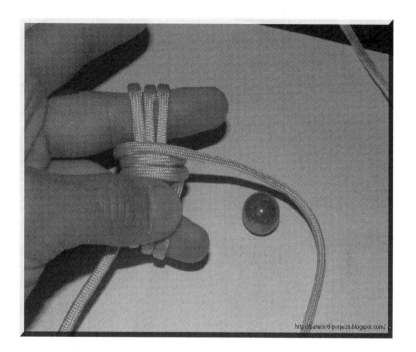

Step three:

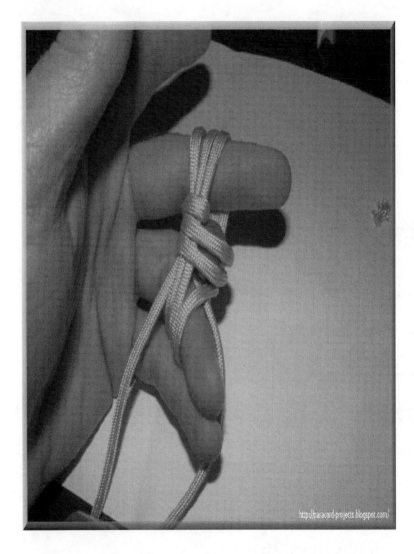

Insert the marble into the middle at this point.

4th step:

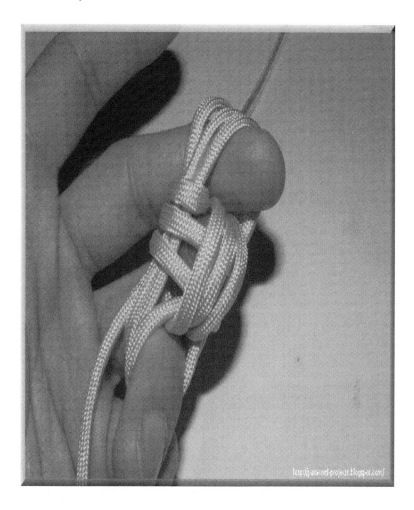

Prior to beginning the tightening process, double check that you have an even cord on all sides.

In my case, I should have a marble cover on each side three times.

5th step:

This is the final stage; from here, you must begin tightening the rope. Simply remember to tighten gradually and not to pull too hard on the initial few tightenings.

When it becomes difficult to draw the cord, use the pointed object.

Often, it's a matter of trial and error to determine how many times we need to wrap the paracord around an object to achieve the desired cover.

It may also be determined by the paracord's thickness.

Sixth step

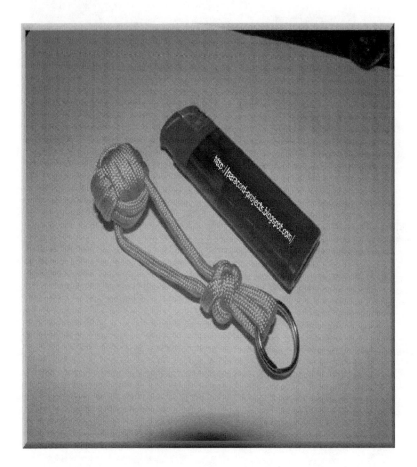

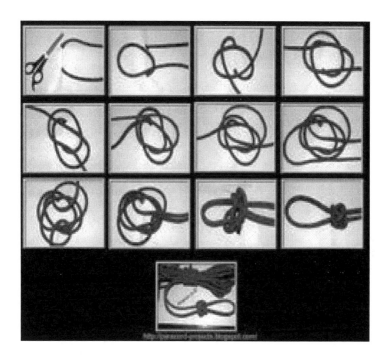

At this point, you have several options for ending the monkey fist; you can tie a basic knot, a snake knot, a diamond knot, or any other method; you can find an instruction for the diamond knot here.

1. Form a diamond knot (see guide image).

2. Before tying the knot, insert the two end cords. (see highlighted image).

3. Trim the ends of the two cords near to the knot.

4. A lighter, a glass of water to dip your finger in (during the fusing process), and a pointed instrument to press the warm rope into the knot.

Begin by fusing the two end cords together; strive to do so neatly and gently to achieve a lovely finish. When both ends are fused, use the lighter to gently warm them and insert them into the knot. Now you can attach a ring to it (or before) and tighten the ring and the bottom two cords.

Option 2, Monkey Fist Guide, Step 7

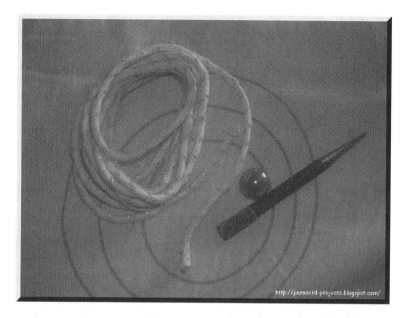

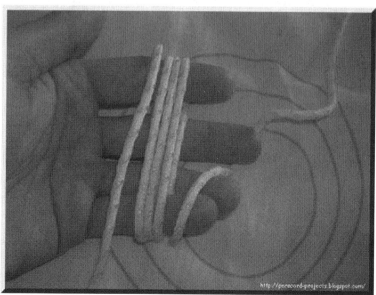

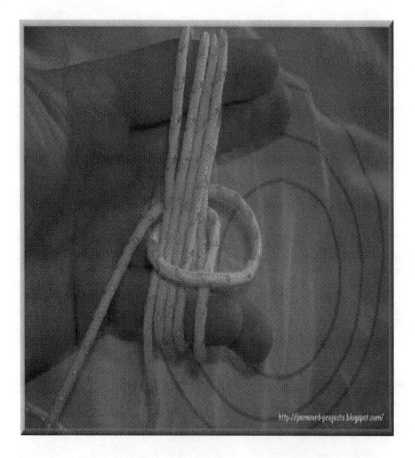

I'm simply demonstrating another way to hold the rope between the fingers in this guide.

Try both methods and determine which is more comfortable for you. This method is more convenient for larger marbles in my opinion.

Additionally, I propose the use of a pointed object. I opted on my nail punch.

Once the knot is completed, the sharp object will assist you in tightening the knot around the marble by drawing the cord.

Guide for Step 8: "Easy Monkey Fist"

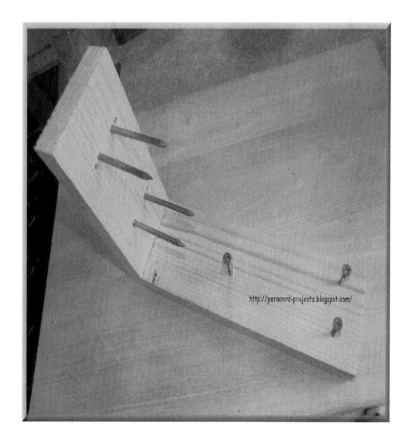

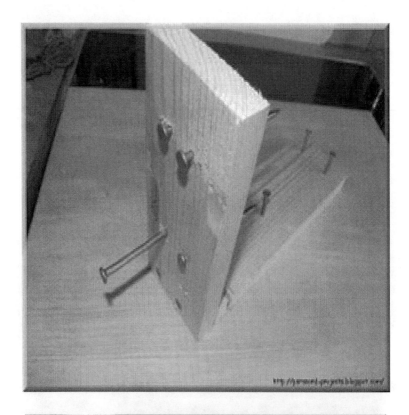

I was thinking that not everyone finds it easy to tie the monkey fist knot between two fingers, so I created this do-it-yourself aid that I call the "Easy Monkey Fist." All that is required is to properly wrap the cable in the monkey fist knot and then remove and tighten it.

It is constructed entirely of scrap timber (L-shaped pieces screwed together) with 4" nails. I bored holes with a diameter similar to that of a nail so that the nails could be easily removed / pulled out.

The little opening at the base is used to secure the start cord.

3 screws (optional) to secure the base to a solid surface.

Drilling a few additional holes is optional to accommodate varied marble/small ball sizes.

I attempted it several times and it took me only a few minutes to form a perfect monkey's fist.

Simply remember to tighten gradually and not to pull too hard on the initial few tightenings.

I used a huge marble in this instruction, and six laps around was sufficient to cover it.

Additionally, keep in mind that the larger the main object is, the more paracord you will use, as well as additional cord for final finishing: snake knot, cobra knot, etc'.

Step 9: Monkey Fist with Golf Ball and Tennis Ball

I acquired some 8mm rope today and decided to construct a Giant monkey fist utilizing a golf ball as the center. Making a monkey fist using thicker cord is much easier.

Increasing in size with the tennis ball.

Step 10: Exchange of Gifts - Paracord

I created a few paracord ties for my Gift Exchange match nepheron in this section.

From left to right:

1. a little monkey fist with a marble center and a snake knot.

2. Combination of a snake knot with a diamond knot.

3. Combination of square and diamond knots.

4. Diamond knot with cobra and knig cobra knots.

5. Bracelet with a cobra knot for survival. I kept the end cord unattached so that nepheron can adjust it to fit his wrist.

6. Large monkey fist (large marble) and Giant monkey fist starting at ten millimeters

CONGRATULATION

Made in the USA
Columbia, SC
23 June 2024

37433113R00087